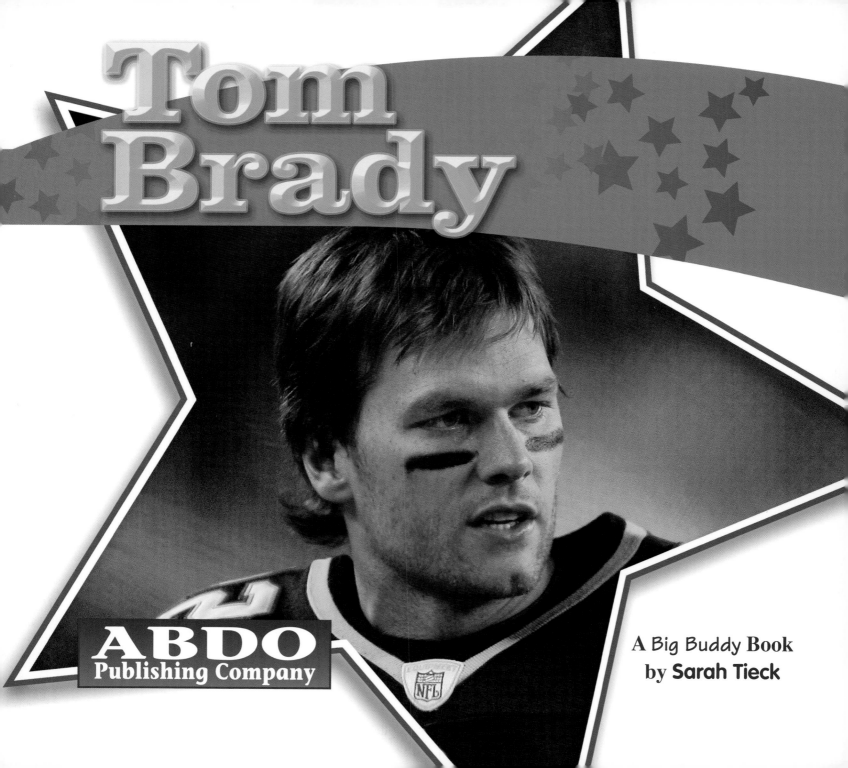

Tom Brady

ABDO
Publishing Company

A Big Buddy Book
by **Sarah Tieck**

VISIT US AT
www.abdopublishing.com

Published by ABDO Publishing Company, 8000 West 78th Street, Edina, Minnesota 55439.

Printed in the United States.

Coordinating Series Editor: Rochelle Baltzer
Contributing Editors: Heidi M.D. Elston, Megan M. Gunderson, Marcia Zappa
Graphic Design: Maria Hosley
Cover Photograph: AP Photo: Winslow Townson
Interior Photographs/Illustrations: AP Photo: Henny Ray Abrams (pages 7, 23), Elise Amendola (pages 15, 27, 29), Duane Burleson (page 11), Peter Cosgrove (page 25), Olivia Hanley (page 17), Lenny Ignelzi (page 25), Dave Martin (page 21), Doug Mills (page 19), Carlos Osorio (page 13), Paul Sancya (page 4), Steven Senne (page 17), Mark J. Terrill (page 25), Winslow Townson (page 23), Kathy Willens (page 19); Getty Images: Bruce Bennet Studios (page 9), WireImage/James Devaney (page 26), AFP/David Maxwell (page 9); Photos.com (page 11).

Library of Congress Cataloging-in-Publication Data

Tieck, Sarah, 1976-
  Tom Brady / Sarah Tieck.
     p. cm. -- (Big buddy biographies)
  Includes index.
  ISBN 978-1-60453-118-3
  1. Brady, Tom, 1977- 2. Football players--United States--Biography--Juvenile literature. 3. Quarterbacks (Football)--United States--Biography--Juvenile literature. I. Title.

GV939.B685T54 2009
796.332092--dc22
[B]

2008009365

Contents

As quarterback, Tom is very important to his team. Quarterbacks are known for their passing skills. They often help the team score.

Football Star

Tom Brady is famous for his sports skills. He is a popular football player for the New England Patriots. Tom has received many awards for his accomplishments.

Many people say Tom is one of the best National Football League (NFL) quarterbacks ever!

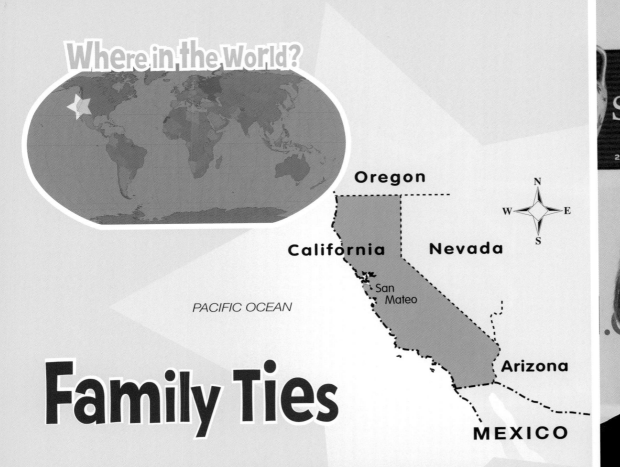

Where in the World?

Oregon

California

Nevada

San Mateo

PACIFIC OCEAN

Arizona

MEXICO

N W E S

Sports Illustrated
SPORTSMAN
of the YEAR
2005 AWARD CELEBRATION

Family Ties

Thomas Edward Patrick "Tom" Brady Jr. was born on August 3, 1977, in San Mateo, California. His parents are Galynn and Tom Brady Sr. Tom has three older sisters named Maureen, Julie, and Nancy.

Tom was named after his father. He went by the name "Tommy" when he was growing up.

Growing Up

During his school years in San Mateo, Tom loved sports. He was good at baseball. But, he really wanted to play football.

Tom watched quarterback Joe Montana play football on television. Joe was one of Tom's role models.

Joe Montana *(left)* is in the Pro Football Hall of Fame. In 1982, Tom watched Joe's famous pass to Dwight Clark. This well-known play *(above)* is called "The Catch."

San Mateo is near San Francisco Bay. The Golden Gate Bridge is a famous San Francisco Bay landmark.

School Years

In 1995, Tom graduated from Junípero Serra High School in San Mateo. Then, he attended the University of Michigan.

There, Tom was on the football team. But in his first two years, he didn't play much. Tom felt let down because he wanted to play more.

Tom first played on a football team as a high school freshman. Eventually he became a quarterback for the University of Michigan.

Soon, Tom got to play more often on the Michigan team. When quarterback Brian Griese graduated, his spot on the team opened up. Tom won the position of starting quarterback.

Tom helped his team win many games. They even won the Citrus Bowl and the Orange Bowl! Bowl games are played after the regular season. Teams are selected to play in them.

Drew Henson, Jason Kapsner, and Tom Brady were Michigan's quarterbacks in 1999. Tom was starting quarterback for most games.

13

Going Pro

When Tom graduated, he wanted to play **professional** football. He was part of the 2000 NFL **draft**. However, Tom was not one of the first players chosen. He was number 199! The New England Patriots chose him.

At first, NFL coaches did not realize what a good player Tom was. But years later, he is considered a great steal for the Patriots.

In 2000, Drew Bledsoe was the starting quarterback for the Patriots. That season, Tom was one of many backup quarterbacks. Soon, he became Drew's number one backup!

Then in 2001, Drew was badly hurt in a game. Afterward, Tom became the team's starting quarterback.

After Drew was injured, he became Tom's backup quarterback.
They worked together until Drew left the team.

Did you know...

At 24, Tom was the youngest starting quarterback to ever win the Super Bowl. The Super Bowl is the championship game of the NFL.

Super Bowl Winner

In 2002, the Patriots beat the Pittsburgh Steelers in a **play-off championship** game. This meant the Patriots would play in the 2002 Super Bowl.

On February 3, the Patriots played the St. Louis Rams. Most people believed the Rams would win. But, the Patriots scored the winning **field goal** as the clock ran out!

Tom was named the 2002 Super Bowl Most Valuable Player.

The Patriots also played in the 2004, 2005, and 2008 Super Bowls. They won in 2004 and 2005! In 2004, Tom was named the Super Bowl Most Valuable Player (MVP).

Every year, the team that wins the Super Bowl receives a Vince Lombardi Trophy. Vince Lombardi was a well-known football coach. He coached the team that won the first two Super Bowls.

Awesome Talent

Tom works hard to improve his skills. He has set many records.

In 2003 and 2004, Tom helped the Patriots win 21 games in a row! This was the NFL's longest winning streak.

People noticed Tom's talent. In 2005, *Sports Illustrated* magazine named him Sportsman of the Year.

Tom threw 50 touchdown passes in the 2007 season. This set an NFL record!

A Famous Life

Tom is known around the world for his football skills. His picture is often in magazines and newspapers. And, there are many stories about his personal life.

Tom wore a special suit to be part of a football video game *(left)*. He has also appeared in public events. These include Disney World parades *(above)* and television shows such as the ESPY Awards *(right)*.

Tom is famous, but he likes to do normal things. He especially enjoys spending time with friends and family.

Tom has a son, John Edward Thomas Moynahan. John was born on August 22, 2007.

When Tom is not playing football, he may spend time alone *(left)*. But, Tom also likes to help others. So, he sometimes appears at charity events *(right)*.

BEST B

Buzz

The 2007 season was one of Tom's best. The Patriots won a record number of games. And Tom received many honors.

Tom and the Patriots continue to set goals. Fans look forward to watching Tom Brady continue to succeed.

The New York Giants beat the Patriots in the 2008 Super Bowl. This was a big surprise! Most people thought Tom and the Patriots would win the game.

Snapshot

★**Name**: Thomas Edward Patrick Brady Jr.

★**Birthday**: August 3, 1977

★**Birthplace**: San Mateo, California

★**Home**: Boston, Massachusetts

★**Turned professional**: 2000

★**Plays with**: New England Patriots

★**Position**: Quarterback

★**Number**: 12

Important Words

championship a game or a match held to find a first place winner.

draft an event during which sports teams choose beginning players.

field goal a way to score three points in football by kicking the ball over a goal post.

play-off a series of games leading to a final match to find a winner.

professional (pruh-FEHSH-nuhl) working for money rather than for pleasure.

Web Sites

To learn more about Tom Brady, visit ABDO Publishing Company on the World Wide Web. Web sites about Tom Brady are featured on our Book Links page. These links are routinely monitored and updated to provide the most current information available.

www.abdopublishing.com

Index